GW01269767

BEYOND ASCENSION 2012:
UNIVERSAL TRUTH
Second Edition

As told by Master Saint Aloysius

BY VICTORIA COCHRANE

Beyond Ascension 2012: Universal Truths
Author: Victoria Cochrane
Tasmania, Australia
ABN: 58 759 564 318
First Printed Balboa Press 2013
Reprinted 2016 Victoria Cochrane Publications
Category: New Age Publications; Ascension; the Universe.
Copyright © Victoria Cochrane

Edited by Victoria Cochrane.
Cover/interior graphics designed by Renea Stubbs.
Printed and bound by Lightening Source, Australia.
Distributed by Ingram Spark.

Cochrane, Victoria, 1960 –
www.victoriacochrane.com
http://victoriacochrane44.com
http://messagesfromotherworlds.blogspot.com
Email: victoriacochrane44@gmail.com
ISBN: 978-1-4525-1092-7

VICTORIA COCHRANE
publications

To Mum and Dad,
Thank you for everything and all
the opportunities you gave me.
I love you and am so thankful
to have you as my parents.

To David and Sally,
Two beautiful souls on
Two different journeys.
May your journeys be joyful,
Your lights shine ever bright,
And the love you give so unconditionally
To others come back to you in abundance.
I am blessed to call you my brother and sister.

CONTENTS

Part Four
The Etheric Realms

ACKNOWLEDGEMENTS

6/8/15

This book came into being when my first book was still in production. Thank you to Moses who came in to give me the message that a second book was being given to me to bring to the world. Many thanks to Master Saint Aloysius who has channelled the content through me and who patiently clarified or repeated the messages when I needed confirmation. Many blessings and thanks also to the Masters of the Cosmic Council who gave me the gift of the Book of Universal Knowledge to assist in the writing of this book. They have been a never-ending support to me and are always there to advise, counsel and love me unconditionally. Most importantly, thank you so much to Creator-Of-All-That-Is, whose presence and love is the foundation on which I move forward in this spiritual journey with purpose, trust and absolute faith.

I give thanks and blessings to my beautiful husband, Richy, who loves me unconditionally and allows me to follow my path and passion with love and commitment. Love and thanks, also, to my beautiful sister, Sally, who has embraced my spiritual journey to encompass her family and circle of friends. I give thanks and blessings to my spiritual family — in particular Jullie, Rose, Robyn, Kelli, Renea, Janelle, Andie, Kelli, Angie, Reiny and Angela whose encouragement, support and love have helped me to continue with confidence and faith in my own abilities. I would also like to thank my new friend, Jamie, who gave his time unconditionally to help me to proof-read and edit my first edition.

This second edition was necessary as some of the messages had become outdated. The masters have explained to me that outcomes often change based on the decisions that people make. The road to Ascension is being resisted by many and the veil continues to lift to expose those who have not been in integrity. People continue to awaken and Ascension is happening, despite the resistance and sabotage of certain groups who work in the darkness.

I thank you for purchasing my books and reading the messages from Spirit with an open heart and mind. I wish you many blessings and the love of Creator as you embark or continue on your own spiritual path. I hope that the messages in this book, as well as the previous one, *'Raising the Energies of Mother Earth Towards and After Ascension; The Highest Truth'* Balboa Press (2013), and my latest one, *'The Alignment of the Universe: Messages from Other Worlds,'* (2015, Ingram Spark) will be of some assistance to you in reaching your own inner peace, truth and oneness with God, the Creator of All That-Is.

Victoria Cochrane, 2016.

FOREWORD

It is with great honour that I write a foreword for Victoria Cochrane's second book. Victoria came into my life when I, the student, was ready. She is my spiritual teacher and friend, who radiates unconditional love, courage and wisdom beyond this realm. Her gifts to this world, at this significant time of vibrational change, challenge us to shed the old ways of ego and raise our vibrational harmony to truth and oneness with the whole — to be at one and live an existence with our Mother-Father God, Creator of All-That-Is. Read these words with open minds and pureness of heart. Allow the words to fill your soul with the warmth and love that is intended; and may you be touched and guided with the richness of spiritual truth on your life's journey, as I have been.

Bless You Victoria.

"We are the keepers, the guardians of the light. Let there be no fear of darkness such that only the Truth will prevail. May the pure of heart rejoice in the spoken word of the Truth. May its glorious harmony resonate within the soul of pure love.

You are loved, you are love, be one with love. For so it is."

(The Masters of the Great Cosmic Council)
Janelle McLaren, 2013.

PREFACE

The Birth of Mother Earth

On the 12/12/12 our meditation group met to help Mother Earth to bring in the energies of the Fifth Dimension. After going first to the Crystalline (Lightworker's) grid to recharge ourselves in the new energies, we asked Creator to take us to help the Masters to assist in the opening of the portal through which Mother Earth was to ascend to the Fifth Dimension.

I was met by the Masters of the Cosmic Council. Behind us was Mother Earth, and in front of us was what looked like a dark cloud. I realised that I was looking out at the universe with the beginning of a portal -- reminiscent of a doorway -- swirling and moving in front of me. All of a sudden we were flying into the portal cloud, and we all took a part of it to hold.

Archangels Michael, Raphael and Gabriel began to fly around and around inside the portal, creating a vortex that began to stretch the portal wider as well as deeper into the cosmos. I saw it stretching both ways, towards the Earth and away from it. It looked like a big white tunnel. The Masters, other lightworkers and I were holding the portal as wide as we could. I then became aware of the Earth moving slowly and steadily through the tunnel. I was witnessing the birth of Mother Earth into the New Age! It was an amazing moment.

Mother Earth slid silently past us and then moved steadily upwards until she was sitting above us. She was a bright, turquoise blue. Others in our group who witnessed this said they saw her as a beautiful turquoise crystal with a pink heart beating in the middle of it. I looked behind me and saw the old Mother Earth; she looked dark and old in comparison to the new-born Earth. The image on the cover of my first book, *Raising the Energies of Mother Earth Towards and After Ascension, 2012: The Highest Truth (2013, Balboa Press)*, drawn so beautifully by my lovely friend Renea, is a depiction of this meditation and the moment of the Ascension of the Earth.

The Masters told me that the portal is to remain open for the next year to eighteen months. In order to ascend with Mother Earth, it is essential that humans raise their vibrations above the dramas and density of the Third Dimensional state. Give love, receive love and BE love. That is all we need to do to rise with Mother Earth into the New Age. This is an amazing opportunity — and how beautiful it is.

Victoria Cochrane, 2013.

ABOUT THIS BOOK

This book is a sequel to my first book, *Raising the Energies of Mother Earth Towards and After Ascension, 2012: The Highest Truth (2013, Balboa Press)*. It is completely channelled from Master Saint Aloysius, and is given at this time to assist people to assimilate their energies to ascend with Mother Earth to the Fifth Dimension. Master Aloysius, who belongs to the same order of masters as the members of the Great Cosmic Council, explains in simple but clear terms how to bring in the lightbody to assimilate your vibrations with that of Mother Earth. He also explains aspects of spirituality that may be new or unclear to many, but which are deemed by the Creator and the Masters as important for people to know.

Third Dimensional (3D) energy is that of the human ego. It is a state of *doing*: of materialism, living in the physical body and of serving self. The Fourth Dimensional state is one of *becoming* and of moving to the Fifth Dimension. If you are feeling more aware of and wary of 3D dramas such as celebrity status, trivial fiction and petty jealousies, while at the same time feeling more empathy towards others and being more aware of looking after the Earth, it is likely you have moved into the Fourth Dimension.

Fifth Dimensional energy is a state of *being* and that of Ascension. People who have reached this level radiate light and unconditional love. They see beyond the dramas of the Earthly Plane and are able to accept people for who they are without judgement. They serve without the need to serve their own egos. They are well on the way to enlightenment and are the way-showers for those who are still struggling to raise their vibrations above the Third Dimension. These people are quite often spiritual teachers, mentors and tireless workers for the planet and humanity.

We are on a never-ending soul-journey of learning, growth and evolvement that leads to oneness and enlightenment. The messages in this book are not aligned with any religion — they are designed to assist people to understand truths about the universe and man's spirituality which human consciousness has previously rejected or misinterpreted. Again, the Masters and I ask that you read this book with an open mind and heart, connecting to your higher, ethereal self that understands universal knowledge in a way that your human mind does not.

The Creator of All-That-Is has no gender. He/She is pure light, truth and unconditional love. He/She is a father-mother God. However, for the sake of fluidity and consistency, all references to the Creator in this book are in the masculine. The words used in this text to refer to the Creator are 'Creator of All That-Is', 'the Creator', 'Creator', 'Source', and 'God'.

Blessings and light,
Victoria Cochrane

PART ONE

CONNECTION TO THE CREATOR

CHAPTER 1

Heat

The heat of the sun warms us every day. It keeps us alive and helps all things to grow. The heat in our bodies is our life force; it keeps our organs alive. It radiates from us and can warm others needing shelter from the cold. Heat is a life-force protector, but too much heat can destroy life. Without water heat will kill rather than nourish. When combined, heat and water give life and promote growth.

The sun is a sacred life force that has many meanings in ancient history. Its symbolism is strong in many cultures. Together with water, which is also sacred, the heat from the sun is a powerful attractor of life. The universe itself does not need heat or water, but humans and other life forms do. God has given life to Earth for a purpose. To live and learn in human or animal form is a gift for the souls who inhabit the universal planes of existence, Earth being one of them. Combined with God's love, all energy forms are in a constant state of creation as well as constantly creating new life. As life creates life, death also follows as it is the natural cycle of the universe.

As we radiate heat, we radiate life. All life comes from the Creator and all life returns to the Creator when it dies. Life and death are a continuous cycle of return. In death we continue our life as a soul who is on a never-ending journey of knowledge and growth. We seek life on Earth so we may learn to grow after death. In truth, there is no death of the human soul which lives on when the body has turned to dust. Heat and water keep the body alive, but the spirit is nurtured by connection to Source—the one God, Creator of All That Is.

When your soul knows this connection to the Creator food, water and heat are only perfunctory in keeping your body alive. The real nourishment comes from knowing God's love and feeling it in your bones, in your cells and in the core of your being. God's love is the heat of your soul. It is the life force that keeps you forever connected and nurtured as you continue on your journey of the quest for knowledge and soul growth.

Connection to the Creator is as necessary to your soul as water is to your body. If your soul cannot feel this connection and feels only separation you will feel lost, disconnected and unsettled — nothing will feel real or make sense to you. It is not necessary for you to be religious to need a connection to God. God is as much a part of you as your physical body. He is connected to your soul, your spirit and your life. You knew God before you were born — you were a part of his light and one with his breath. To feel separated from him is a devastation your soul cannot recover from. Your soul realizes this whether you believe in God in this lifetime or not. Your soul knows God and his love is the life force that keeps you connected to him, to Mother Earth and to yourself.

And so it is.

CHAPTER 2

Talk, Listen, Pray and Meditate

Talk to God and he will hear you. He will also always answer you — God listens to everyone. He hears you as individuals and also as the masses. He knows every thought and word you speak, he sees every dream and hears every wish.

Creator is with every man, woman and child. He is in everyone and he listens and responds. He weeps when you weep, laughs when you laugh and feels what you feel. Intervention from the Creator is only given when one has asked for it. He cannot impinge upon your free will any more than a human can, as it is against spiritual law. The decisions you make are yours to be borne, but if you wish to ask for assistance or advice from the Creator He will always give it.

God speaks in tones of love and wisdom. He speaks through nature and on the winds. Yet if you listen and wait for an answer in your head or in your heart, you will receive it. It may be a thought, an unspoken feeling or a song. However you receive it, He will always answer. God speaks only the truth. The answers you hear may not always be what you have wished for, but they are what He has deemed that you need to know at this point in time. The Creator does not require that you heed His advice; it is up to you. But when you talk to Him and ask for an answer for your highest and best, He will answer you.

Have you listened? Have you heard? God speaks.

Listen, and you will hear.

There are many ways to speak to our Creator and to hear his messages; prayer is but one of them. When you pray you are connecting to God and asking for assistance — you are giving your permission for Him to intervene. Permission is always required before any intervention can be provided — God must abide by the law of non-intervention just as any other ethereal or human being must do. Prayer is not a religious mode of communication, although most humans see it as such. It is a direct communication with God, but it does tend to be a one-way communication as most people do not stop to hear an answer! It may take some practice, but all humans have the ability to hear God's voice — you are all connected and all 'psychic,' as the saying goes; you just do not believe it to be so. Prayer comes in many forms. It is not necessary to be on your knees in a place of worship for your prayers to be heard. God the Creator hears your pleas wherever you are and however you ask. You may be in the car, on a boat or in bed. You may speak to Him out loud, yet he will also hear you if you speak to Him with a thought or in your heart. He will hear you through the angels, through a priest, or through your tears.

God is with you always and there is nothing that He does not know about you. There is also nothing that He does not love about you. Your connection to Creator cannot be broken, even when you have lost your belief or temporarily lost your way. His guidance is ever with you, no matter whether you not recognise it or not. He is in your body and is a part of your soul. You are made in His image and you speak his words. You are no more separated from God than your body is separated from your soul. You are one with Him and infinitely connected.

Many people see meditation as a spiritualist form of prayer, but it is also a way of being directly connected to God and the *All*. Meditation is another form of prayer, but many who meditate are aware of their connection to God so they wait for the answers to be given. Their connections are therefore strengthened and their psychic and spiritual gifts take form very quickly. *These humans are not special or in any way better than anyone else!* They are merely attuned to their spiritual selves and thus learn to reap the benefits of their connection to the Creator and to the *All*.

Meditation has long been the form of connecting to the *All* that is favoured by those who are in tune with their spiritual selves. They have found a way to always be aware of their connection to God and the

God within. Many people spend a lifetime searching for oneness and the ability to know God, but what if I told you that all you need do is to look within yourself for your soul already knows this state? You may seek a spiritual teacher to guide you in your spiritual quest, but a good teacher will always guide you to look within, to still your mind and to listen for the voice of God, that is also your own voice, telling you the answers you have asked questions to and giving you the answers that you seek. They will empower you to be connected to yourself.

Many call the ability to hear the message of Spirit "channelling," and they attribute this ability to a gifted few. The reality is that all souls born upon the earthly plane can channel the voice of Spirit, whether it be God, an angel, an ascended master or a passed-over loved one. There is no one person on Earth who is more special than another. Those who have learnt to channel are the listeners — they are the ones who have simply stopped to listen, that is all.

In this time after Ascension, as your body assimilates the new energies and becomes aware of its urges to reconnect to Spirit, we the masters ask that you begin to meditate. Take the time to sit in the stillness of your own breath, to feel the beating of your heart and to listen for the voice of God within. Still your chattering mind and simply *be*. Yes, it may take practice. Finding the time may be difficult. *Make* the time however you can, finding your inner connection to Source that you may have forgotten but, in fact, have never lost.

When you reconnect to the voice of God your inner guidance will be strong. What was muddled before will become clear. What seemed impossible will suddenly seem plausible. What was important may become less so and what held no importance before may become more important. What seemed doubtful will reveal its true identity and your own spiritual and psychic abilities will emerge. You will find your true self and you will become one of the listeners. This is a gift from God that is every person's right and every person's gift.

The voice of the Creator is always available to those who take the time to listen. When you pray or meditate His message can be heard in a breath, as a voice, as a feeling, a colour or as an image. When you ask for guidance He will always give it. It will perhaps not come in a way that was expected, for the way of God is wise and His guidance will be given in a way that each individual will understand. Do not fear God or His voice. Do not fear the psychic ability that is within you. It is up to you whether you choose to use it and to listen, but when you do you will know your connection to the Creator and that all humans are special and equal in the eyes of God. You are all connected and you can all hear Him. You must simply believe it is so and then stop to listen.

It is that simple.

CHAPTER 3

The Sacred Breath

The breath of God is eternal. It gives life and it sustains every living thing through life. Every breath you take brings you closer to death. This is not a threat or a promise, but merely the reality of life. Therefore it is recommended that you breathe with intention and with love, because the breath in your body is your life force and the connection to all that is sacred and pure.

Each breath connects you to the sacred elements of air and earth. It holds you to life and keeps you grounded on the earthly plane. Air is sacred because of its connection to Earth and to life, and earth is sacred because it sustains and brings life forth (please refer to the chapter, 'Air', p.59 in *Raising the Energies of Mother Earth Towards and After Ascension 2012: The Highest Truth,' Second Edition, Cochrane, 2016*).

You are one with God every minute of every day. The air that you breathe contains God's essence in tiny particles called *adamantine* particles. These particles bring with them the message from Creator that you are loved and *one* with Him. You are the life force that brings His love to the Earth and to all with whom you come into contact. When you breathe in the adamantine particles of creation and breathe them out with loving intention you are doing God's work, because you are sending healing energy to the Earth. You are also connecting to the sacred wisdom of the universe, because every adamantine particle contains the universal mind of God which is all-knowing and wise to the intricate ways of the laws of the universe.

The sacred breath is a powerful way of connecting your life force to the Creator's energy and of bringing love and pure healing light to Earth. It will also assist you in your own healing and raising of vibrations towards Ascension and enlightenment. It can be done each day and is a beneficial practice, both for you and for the planet.

Follow these simple directions to send healing light and love to the Earth through the sacred breath:

❖ Ground your energy through your heartspace down to Mother Earth and see the light of Creator in your mind's eye.

❖ Breathe in air as light on a count of four.

❖ Hold the light and breath in your heart-space, then, on another count of four, breathe the light out as love.

❖ See the world in your mind's eye and send this breath of love out to it with the highest and best of intentions.

❖ Do not just fill your lungs when you breathe; rather fill your whole body with the sacred breath of life. Feel it in your abdomen, your chest, your legs, and your heart.

❖ Breathe it out from the top of your lungs to your feet, then breathe it out with love and joy.

❖ To assist in your own healing, breathe the light in with the intention of clearing, balancing or healing a part of your body or an area of your life. Send the light to the area and breathe out anything that no longer serves you.

❖ To access the universal mind, (please refer to Chapter 6, 'The Universal Mind' (p.27) in' The Alignment of the Universe: Messages from Other Worlds, (Cochrane, 16, Victoria Cochrane Publications) hold the adamantine particles in your lungs and see them with your third eye. Ask your question or hold the intention of accessing universal wisdom for your highest and best. Continue to breathe in light and love as you hold the energy in your sacred heart space (refer to p. 41).

Bring your light and love to the world as God's light and love. Feel the shift in your consciousness as you know oneness and peace. When your consciousness shifts it will begin to shift in others; when you love others you allow them to love you. Peace will begin to fill you and those around you. The beginning of real peace on Earth resulting in ascension and oneness depends upon all humans sending light and love to themselves, their fellow man and to the planet.

And so it is.

CHAPTER 4

Jesus

Jesus sends his love to you through your heart-space. He sends healing by touching your soul with his light and with God's love. He is the messenger. He is a way to God's light, because he shows you how to live in the light and how to raise your energies to *be* the light for others.

It was never intended that Jesus take the place of God or for him to be the object of worship. His light and love showed the world how it is possible to live in service to others, for he was always in service and forever remains so. By serving humanity he chose the path of the Master. He walks this path still.

Call to Jesus and he will come. Ask him for healing and he will give it. Show him your broken heart and he will heal it. Send him to others and he will go. Speak to him and he will answer. Touch him and he will return your touch, hold him and he will hold you — he is in service to you and will always answer your call.

Jesus does not sit on a throne: he walks amongst you every day, working to save the planet and all of those who dwell upon it. He works tirelessly as a master and a servant of God to bring the Creator's light to the world. He will work with you and heal you, but only if you want him to. You must always ask, and then he will come.

Let go of religion. Let go of the mandate that Jesus is the only way to redemption. Heed not the Christian who warns of impending doom or life in Hell; there is no such thing and no devil either, unless you choose to live in that reality. The devil in your mind is your human ego, as the choices you make create the life that you live — the thoughts that you think create your reality. Do not blame any devil, nor must you blame God for your misfortunes. He shows you the way that will serve you the best, but should you choose otherwise the consequences are of your own making.

Creator loves you unconditionally and makes no judgement for what you choose. He does not send Jesus to force you to see the light. The way is always open, should you choose it. No doors are ever closed, no way is ever wrong. Let Jesus into your heart and you will know great joy and boundless love. But, make not the mistake that he is God or that he is tied to religion. Religion is not required to know the love of Jesus or to feel the bounty of God's love.

Christ came to Earth with the intention of saving humans from their sins. He was of the light and a way to the light.* He never wavered from this task. His mission was simple — to show the world how much God loves you and that to love God is to love yourself, because you and God are one and the same.

Jesus left the Earth as he came: one with the light and of the light. His forgiveness was absolute and ever-encompassing. Man rejoiced at his coming and mourned his passing, and has forever bourn him on a pedestal as the one-and-only saviour. He is revered for his sacrifice, and his birth and death are re-played year after year.

It is time to move on from Jesus' sacrifice, for the *second coming* is not as Christians perceive. Jesus walks the Earth as a master on the etheric plane, and aspects of his soul are incarnated in many humans walking on this Earth, as is the case with every master who ever lived life as a human. Jesus is not reincarnating once again — His *coming* is not what is to save the planet. It is time for the world to realise that the only way to save the Earth has occurred — she has ascended. Jesus and the great masters have been unerring in their quest for this occurrence, and they work tirelessly still, assisting all of those who wish to raise their vibrations to do so.

It is not helpful for man to live in the past when the future of the Earth is in jeopardy. Mother Earth was dying, and her soul cried out for assistance; she could not sustain life on Earth such as it was. On the 12/12/12 she rose to a new dawn and felt fresh air in her lungs.

She had to rise anew to save herself and all who dwelt upon her from extinction. The time for this to happen has passed. This, dear ones, was the *second coming*.

Jesus came to save you. He did so. But now he speaks to you from his heart. He asks you to listen to those who speak of a *new age*, and to believe them, for it is time for the truth to be told and heard. His body has gone to ashes, but his spirit is alive in each and every one of you. He dances in your hearts and he speaks to your consciousness:

"Dear ones, I have arisen. Now it is time for Mother Earth to do the same, and to bring all of her children with her. Rise up from the old ways of thinking. Awaken from your slumber and do what you agreed to do before you were born, which is to embrace this new age as the new way to God. I will show you the way if you need me to. Come to me and we shall go together."

God shines His Light through many on Earth who are the way-showers of the new age. These lightworkers have been given information to tell the world of the changes that have been nigh for centuries. Up until now the believers have been few and the naysayers have been many. But, as the Earth sank ever lower into corruption and greed, the veil lifted and the new age became a reality. The Age of Aquarius is here and it is time to awaken from your slumber. It is time for the *second coming*, and how joyous it is.

And so it is.

---

*   For more information on the true story of Jesus, see references listed in the bibliography.

PART TWO

ASCENSION

CHAPTER 5

The New Age

The new age is upon us, and many of you are shaken. You have awoken to energy that is new and to hearts that are pure. What it means or how it affects you is unknown to you, and so this book is given to explain it all to you.

The ascension of Mother Earth is not a new concept — it has been in the planning for many centuries, before the Mayans formed their Calendar of the Ages. They foretold of many things that have since come true and this event that is unfolding before us is but another of their prophecies that are now coming to light. Ascension is not a dream or a fairy tale, nor is it a lie told to scare the masses — there have been too many of those. Ascension is a reality that is set to awaken the world to a new consciousness and to bring it into alignment with powerful cosmic forces that vibrate at a much higher frequency. There will be no room for darkness in a world ablaze with light. This, beloveds, is a time of great rejoicing.

Every human is a Light-Being. You all came from the light and you will go back to the light when you die. Your souls knew only love before you were born and you incarnated on Earth with the intention of spreading your love and light to all you came across. Children manage to stay in the light for a time, but by the time they are adults the light has faded and many become Earth-bound beings who are stuck in the drudgery of day-to-day living. We have spoken before of life on Earth being the way to soul evolvement, and so it is, but even so, life on Earth is hard for many for whom living in the light has become an unattainable dream and an unimaginable reality.

The way to Ascension is to allow the bringing in of your Lightbody so you may rise once again to the etheric state of being that you were in before you were born. The Lightbody is your etheric body and it will bring your energies back up to the highest vibration that you can comfortably maintain on Earth — the Fifth Dimensional state.

The Fifth Dimension is the ultimate state, one of *being*, not *doing* which is the Third Dimensional state many humans are still living in on Earth. In order to ascend without feeling sickness or disequilibrium it is essential for you to leave the Third Dimension and to raise your vibrations through the Fourth Dimension, which is the state of *becoming*, until you are vibrating high enough to ascend into the Fifth Dimension.

When you are in, or even working towards, a Fifth-Dimensional state you will be more able to remove yourself from the dramas of the Third Dimension. You will no longer engage in gossip, nor will you care for trivia or anything that holds no importance for you. You will be able to see things from other people's perspectives and you will be much less judgmental of others overall. You will find that meditation is necessary to keep you grounded and centred and your higher purpose for being on Earth will be revealed to you. You may begin to help others through healing or teaching, and your feeling of being one with the Earth and the All will intensify.

The new energies are challenging for many and there is continuing resistance as people struggle to find their way through the confusion. Many people around the world may find themselves at a crossroads where important decisions need to be made, perhaps at the sacrifice of a long-lasting relationship. Know that, if something or someone is falling away out of your life there is good reason for it. When you trust that all is as it should be the road to a higher state of *being* will be much easier for you.

Mother Earth has ascended. She cannot hold onto the lower energies of the Third Dimension any longer. Her Third Dimensional state is dying and disintegrating and those caught up in it are like spiders caught in their own webs. To hold onto this state is to agree for your soul to remain stuck and in limbo. Let go and come with us into the new age of the Fifth Dimension, the state of being, the state of unconditional love, oneness, truth and honesty. A new life awaits you, but you must trust and allow yourself to believe it can be so.

We are waiting and we will help you. All you need to do is ask.

And so it is.

CHAPTER 6

Ascension into the Fifth Dimension

The ascended state is a state of consciousness. It is a way of thinking and being at a higher and faster vibration than that of the Third or Fourth Dimensions. To attain this level one must choose to bring in the Lightbody. However, there are also other choices one must make in order to reach the ascended state. Acceptance that ascension has occurred is one choice. Abandonment of Third Dimensional beliefs is another. Many people have chosen not to ascend with Mother Earth. There is no judgement in this decision for all humans have free will. There are, however, consequences for making this decision, for there will be no turning back after Mother Earth has fully ascended.

Not everyone is ready for ascension, although many have ascended already. There are things you need to put into place to reach the state of the Fifth Dimension. To allow for the higher energies of the Lightbody you must raise your consciousness above the lower energies of the masses. That is, you must consciously control your thoughts and monitor your actions in order for them to be positive ones of love and no judgement. This takes considerable effort and practise. There are those on Earth who seek to keep the energies of the Earth in the Third Dimension in order for them to keep control of the minds and the monies of the masses so, for some, rising above the pull of this denser energy will be extremely difficult.

Every thought, word, and deed creates; everything you think, do and say goes out into the universal, human consciousness and creates reality. Whether positive or negative, light or dark, the words, deeds and thoughts of man are all united as one large consciousness that controls the energies of the Earth. Man has been sinking under the load of negative energy that he has created through his judgemental thoughts and vengeful actions. In order to ascend, each person must make a conscious effort to rise above this kind of thinking and doing to one of a higher perspective. Man must remember that he is here on Earth to learn lessons* and that all thoughts, words and actions are lessons in the making. When you can see and remember this your vibrations will already have risen to a higher state.

Love rules the universe. It is all there is; we have spoken of this before at length. God loves all on Earth equally — there is no separation from his love or from Him. Every living thing is part of the *all* — you are one with God and one with Mother Earth. When you know oneness you will know yourself as an image of God and as a co-creator with him. When you love yourself equally to all others, including God, then you will be ready to bring in your Lightbody and ascend to the Fifth Dimension.

Holding a Fifth Dimensional state is not easy and, once you have reached it you must also work to maintain it. Most people who achieve ascension find that they do slip in and out of it at times — one is only human, after all and living in a world of very dense thoughts and vibrations. It is therefore vitally important that people who have brought in their Lightbodies and who are vibrating at a faster rate keep themselves grounded, connected and their chakras clear of Third Dimensional frequencies. This can be achieved in many ways, the most important being regular meditation. Keeping your mind clear of confusion, thinking with your heart and sending love when others send hate are all just the beginning of maintaining an ascended state. Staying out of drama is the key.

Nothing on Earth is ever constant other than the love of the Creator. When you can harness His love and be in it, of it and one with it you will have a much greater chance of maintaining a Fifth Dimensional state.

---

* (refer to Raising the Energies of Mother Earth Second Edition, Cochrane, 2016)

CHAPTER 7

The Winds of Change

Wind is in the trees; it blows across the seas. Winds bring change — in the weather, in the temperature and in moods. There are many changes in the winds: they speak of great change and many events that will or have already, changed lives and the directions of those lives in the future.

Because Mother Earth now sits in the Fifth Dimension her frequencies are higher and her vibrations are faster. She speaks of love and peace, not of hatred and war. Her vibrations will no longer tolerate the foibles of man. It is time for man to step up out of the density of thinking that is the Third Dimension and take the leap of faith to consciously raise his vibrations and become one with Mother Earth.

See this change as it is — as one of saving your planet from extinction. It has been a long time in the planning and has occurred due to a long reign of terror by humankind. We do not say this in jest: the plundering of Mother Earth by your kind has been fierce and rampant. There are those who would protest that they have done all they can to protect her, and we acknowledge this, but it has not been enough.

The changes occurring in your weather patterns of late are no accident, nor are they all brought about from the same source. Many floods are a cleansing of negative energies such as corruption, greed and lies that have been told for personal gain. You cannot hold onto any wealth that has been attained through corruption — these energies cannot be tolerated in the Fifth Dimension. You may feel you were an innocent party caught up in the cleansing, but this is just an unfortunate consequence of the actions of a few that have impacted upon many.

There are dark forces upon the Earth who have been instigating many events that have caused death and destruction to humankind. Their reign of terror is now coming to an end because they cannot stay in the Fifth Dimensional vibrations of Mother Earth. It is not worth dwelling upon their actions because their deeds have come undone and the world has awakened from its slumber. People no longer believe the propaganda fed up to them on a platter, nor will they be led to the slaughter unknowingly any more. The time has come for the darkness to be consumed by the light. It has happened and it is done.

Change is for the better, and it has been a long time in the planning. There is no need to worry that the world will end for after ascension life will continue fairly much as you have known it. Yet, there will be many small changes that will become more noticeable as time wears on. Let us outline some of them here.

The skies will be clearer, the air cleaner and the waterways will sparkle and shimmer more brightly. You will notice that nature will be more vibrant and the colours will seem brighter. The birds will be more vocal and the animals will move with more purpose.

The weather patterns will settle down. There will be less cataclysms such as earthquakes, tornadoes, hurricanes and tsunamis. The rains will come in areas where they have been scarce, and flooded areas will know drier periods and less frequent rains.

There will be less anger and distress amongst humans. Wars will suddenly seem fruitless and will be ceased. Troops will be withdrawn and sent home, truces will be made. Enemies will become allies — uneasy ones at first, but ties will strengthen and bonds formed. The negative energies consuming the human consciousness for so long will begin to transform into positive energies of love, friendship and tolerance. This will occur over a period of time after ascension has occurred.

There will be less poverty and inflation. The financial situation of many families will become more equal. Over time money will be a less important commodity than friendships and relationships. While materialism will always have a place in the minds of men that are ruled by ego, money and possessions will begin to make way for bartering, bargaining, exchanges of mutual benefit and a sharing of resources. People will become much more united in their everyday lives, and a greater sense of belonging and community will ensue.

In the Fifth Dimension you will be happy to just *be*. The daily dramas that have filled your life will no longer hold importance. You will not feel the need to judge others, engage in gossip or to seek vengeance for deeds previously done against you. You will not want to dredge up the past or to worry endlessly about the future. You will be happy to live in the moment and to see your life for what it is: a wonderful opportunity to live, love and learn lessons towards soul evolvement and enlightenment. The Brotherhood of Man will be restored. You will all feel a oneness with each other that you have not felt before. The strengthening of bonds between you will be fierce, and humans will feel a need to protect, not harm, one another.

This is a time of transition of energies. You cannot expect things to change overnight, and the changes that have been described above will be gradual. For a time there will be much resistance and it will seem to many that the Earth's ascension was but a dream. Terrorism and war will intensify and there will be desperate attempts by the darker forces to overshadow the work of the Angelic Realm and the Lightworkers of the world. However, the energies of the new Earth will be felt by all, no matter how high or low one's vibrations are, and the mass awakening of human consciousness will continue. The higher you allow your vibrations to rise, the easier this transition will be for you, and the bigger the difference you will be able to make for Mother Earth and your fellow humans.

Be in a state of love. Feel the Earth as she moves and breathes beneath your feet. Feel her sigh reverberate through your very being. You are one with Mother Earth, as you are with God. Move in harmony and synchronicity and you will feel your energies become as those of Mother Earth — alive, vibrant and renewed.

And so it is.

CHAPTER 8

Bringing in the Lightbody

The Lightbody is your etheric body. It is the state you were in before your birth into a human body. In this state you know only love, and you are one with the universe, with Creator, and the *all*. Your Lightbody vibrates at a much faster rate than that of your physical body which allows you to access etheric knowledge and to assimilate higher energies much more readily. In this state you are in touch with your spiritual self and life on Earth clearly becomes a human experience: the lessons you are learning are all designed to help your soul to evolve to a higher level. Life as a human is merely an illusion because the dramas that play out form the stage on which you learn, grow, and evolve spiritually.

The human form does not just consist of a physical body. You have, in fact, four bodies that impact upon your health and happiness and that harbour feelings and emotions from the past. They are the physical, emotional, mental and causal bodies. When you are in the Third Dimensional state your physical body rules everything. If you are sick you look for a physical cause. However, as you allow your Lightbody, or etheric state, to enter your energy fields you begin to realise that the physical body is just one area that holds pain and, in fact, is the body *least* likely to be holding the cause of the malady.

The physical human body merely reflects what the other bodies of the person are holding. If the emotional body is ill, a symptom will occur in the physical body. If the mental body cannot rest, the physical body will respond with a physical response. If the person's spiritual body has not come to terms with the past or has lost its connection to the *all*, the physical symptoms that occur will have no apparent source.

As your energy fields begin to accept and accommodate the higher energies of the Fifth Dimension your physical body will become more susceptible to environmental factors that are not in sync with the rhythms of your etheric state. Your other bodies will cry out to release all traumas that have gone before because no lower energies or negative memories can remain in an enlightened being. Your physical symptoms may increase dramatically, forcing you to look within to uncover the cause and source of your discomfort. Ask us for assistance in this endeavour and you will be guided to the best way, or person, to help you to release all that no longer serves you so that you can make the transition to your Lightbody more easily.

The Lightbody cannot tolerate vibrations of hatred, anger, intolerance, injustice, racism or inequality. On the etheric planes we know each other as equals and we treat each other with reverence and love. As you bring in your Lightbody you will notice that the dramas played out by those whose vibrations are of a lower order are incomprehensible to you and no longer of any consequence. You will also notice that the wonders of nature and the universe are becoming much more important to you and preserving Mother Earth and all who dwell upon her will be your main desire. One cannot live upon a planet so bountiful without becoming increasingly aware of the precious nature of her cargo. The gift of life cannot be downplayed or ignored. When you are in your Lightbody, or as you are bringing in the higher energies towards this quest, your higher purpose for being on Earth will become clear to you and your connection to Mother Earth, to Creator, and the *all* will be eternally strengthened. Most of all you will know what it is to dwell in peace and harmony, and you will become a way-shower for others. This is the way of enlightenment, and the only way to truly achieve peace on Earth.

Blessings and light to you, Dear Ones.

And so it is.

CHAPTER 9

Gifts

The gifts of Mother Earth are many and man reaps the rewards of her bounty. He uses her resources and bleeds them dry. However, many of you treasure her gifts and are protectors rather than destroyers. To protect Mother Earth is to respect her sacredness, which in turn shows respect to oneself, for you are a sacred being of light who is undergoing a human experience. Life is sacred and must be nurtured and protected.

There are agreements on Earth between man and animals. Some animals have agreed to give themselves to man for food. This is a true gift of nature and continues now after ascension. To kill for food is a natural cycle of evolution, but it is necessary to give thanks and blessings for the gifts provided to you in order to maintain or raise their vibrations to the highest nutritional level. If you do not give thanks for the gifts of the Earth, the vibrations of the food will be lower and your body will not gain the benefits that were intended.

All life, whether human, animal, or plant, has a consciousness. The smallest life form on Earth still breathes in the Creator-essence of life. *All* life is sacred, no matter how small or insignificant it may seem. Each insect, each creature, each plant and each person are living and pulsating with the Creator's life force within them. To take a life without permission or a blessing is an impingement upon freedom, and the energy that is returned to you will be tainted as a result.

All gifts are freely given. Mother Earth gives up her bounty with joy and abandonment, but she expects the returns to be ones of respect and sustainability. Every gift has its limits, and every life form must be allowed to replenish itself and to continue its evolutionary path. No form of life should be allowed to become extinct. There should be enough for everyone to share without greed exceeding need.

Take the gifts that are offered to you, always giving thanks and showing gratitude for receiving them. Reward Mother Earth by replenishing her stocks and allowing time for re-growth of what you take. Plundering will only lead to destruction and imbalance. Where life can be left alone allow it to live. All creatures and life forms have a place in the garden of Mother Earth, which is part of the *all* and is God–given.

And so it is.

CHAPTER 10

Protecting the New Energies

The new age has brought with it new conditions for living on the Earth. It is no longer appropriate to living in the energy of *doing for self* and stroking the ego. It is time for the human soul to look beyond his own self's needs and to consider the needs of his fellow man. The years following ascension are a time of assimilating new energies on Earth. Those who have already ascended find themselves living between worlds: that is, they know how to look at things from the higher perspective of the Fifth Dimension, yet they are also living in the lower energies of non-ascended, less-enlightened beings. It is therefore a time of assimilating the higher energies into the day-to-day living on Earth. Ascended beings must continue to communicate with their fellow humans in order to assist as many people as possible to bring in their Lightbodies and to ascend into the Fifth Dimension.

The denser energies of the Third Dimension are now falling away. Any person or situation that is not in integrity will begin to be exposed. Lies and untruths will be revealed, and long-hidden secrets will be unveiled. What has previously been hidden will be stripped away to reveal bare bones: the skeletons in the cupboard, as you say. Know that this must occur, because the higher energies of the Fifth Dimension cannot tolerate the lower energies that have ruled the Earth in the Third Dimensional state.

When Mother Earth rose to the Fifth Dimension she brought with her the promise of a future no longer steeped in hatred. Humans who rose with her can no longer tolerate the egos of those who tell

31

them that they are better than others, that they know more, or that the needs or status of some are better than others. The illusion of separation is no more, as those who have ascended now practise oneness, peace, tolerance, and unconditional love. They see things from a higher perspective, aware of the reasons for the actions that impinge upon others and helping their fellow humans to feel love and forgiveness rather than hatred and the seeking of revenge. When Lightworkers practise these things in the presence of others the ripple effect is great. Mother Earth is supporting those who share her higher energies, and is willing those who do not to step into her higher vibrations to do so in order to progress towards enlightenment.

The new energies are still unstable and fragile. They are affecting all upon Earth, including those who have brought in their Lightbodies and who are vibrating at a faster rate. Relationships that served you once will begin to fall away. Pursuits you once enjoyed will suddenly seem trivial and no longer important. Items in the news will be irritating because of their irrelevance. People who cannot see beyond their own self will be less tolerable to you, though it will be easier to show them tolerance and to excuse their behaviour. Where once there would have been arguments there will be more forgiveness and frankness without aggression.

However, there continues to be much disequilibrium amongst humans as the energies of the Earth are adjusting. More and more humans are leaving the planet altogether as they cannot tolerate the injustices of the human race any longer. There is much violence as peoples' energies are disrupted and this will continue for as long as these people need to decide whether they will listen to the promise of ascension and to put their faith in the new age or not. If they do not there will be consequences, for as the consciousness of the old Earth crumbles and dies, the new consciousness cannot take flight under the weight of resistance and oppression. The new energies will continue to strengthen and conflict with the dense energies of the Third Dimension, bringing great discomfort, confusion and renewed conflict amongst humans. The resulting slowing down of the ascension process could mean that its effects will not be enough to save those who have chosen to resist it and there could be a mass exiting of human life from the planet in a series of calamitous world events and singular acts of violence.

The new energies are strong and are causing discomfort for many, but we ask you to persist and to make every effort to keep your energy fields clear so that the new energies can assimilate into your body. The more you do the higher your vibrations will be and living upon the renewed Mother Earth will be a great joy. The time it takes for ascension to fully integrate upon the Earth will depend upon the decisions people make to engage with and invest their energies into the process. It may take years or it may take decades. The longer it takes the less likely it is to ever fully integrate, and this would be the greatest calamity of all. Now, whenever 'now' is for you, is the best time and the greatest opportunity you will ever have of changing your perspective and of raising your energies, thus changing your life and the world around you.

The ascension process is a beautiful opportunity for man to rise up out of the negative energies that have been dominant in the past. The new energies must be nurtured, revered, and protected in order for the new age to be one of unconditional love, oneness, and peace for all. It can only happen when each and every individual makes the conscious commitment to do so.

And so it is.

PART THREE

THE SOUL

CHAPTER 11

Speaking to the Soul

Your soul knows oneness and it knows God. It knows who you are in Spirit and the path you chose before you were born. Your soul speaks to you in a way that your mind does not understand but which your body does. The body responds to soul-speak through happiness, health and well-being, or through unspeakable sadness, illness and grief. When you carry negative messages from your soul your body responds with pain, sickness, cancer, or even death.

You are all on a soul journey. Most of you have lived many lives. You have travelled far afield and have had many experiences. You have known life and death, love and hatred, agony and ecstasy. You have made life-long friendships and have also known unbearable loneliness. Your lives and loves have been both torturous and ones of joyful abandonment. Your soul knows many truths and harbours many lies. It knows oneness and it also knows separation. It knows grief, despair, joy, pain, guilt, and humour. It knows who you are and why you are here even if your conscious mind does not.

Your soul is not your spirit. Your spirit is your essence it is the part of you that is connected to God and eternal life. It is your connection to your past lives and the etheric realms. Your spirit is your nature: it is who you are. Your soul bears your spirit on its onwards journey, ever evolving and learning, looking for ways to mastery and enlightenment. Your soul is your star-ship, your vehicle that takes you on your continuous journey through life and death. It is your vehicle for learning, for growth and for the gaining of truth.

Listen to your soul. It speaks to you in ways all four of your bodies understand. It tells you if it is carrying pain, sorrow, guilt or grief, anger or hurt. Your past journeys are with you they are part of who you are. Respect the emotions and traumas associated with these journeys, acknowledge them then let them go. When you do this your physical body will respond. If you have been sick you may begin to feel better, or you may find that the illness will vanish altogether. If you have had pain it may subside or disappear. It will seem amazing, but when you listen to what your emotional, mental or causal body has been saying to you your physical body will respond accordingly.

It is not always easy to find the emotional cause of physical pain; you may need some help to do so from one who is tuned in to their own psychic abilities. However, you will be surprised at how much will be released by just acknowledging that there is more to your illness than a physical cause. So, if you have ailments which no practitioner can find a cure for, the physical body is not where you should be looking to find the cause.

The past is not haunting you for it has formed who you are in the present, yet it can sometimes be a blockage to your way forward. When any of your bodies carry memories from another time they have the power to trigger physical symptoms that have no likely cause. One can therefore carry pain and discomfort for years that no medical practitioner can diagnose. You need to look further. In addition, if you have not learnt your lessons from the past or released the trauma of past events, your soul will continue to carry them until they are acknowledged and released. This could take many years or many lifetimes.

Your causal body knows your soul journey and your spiritual essence. It is your etheric body which is always in touch with Spirit. Your mental body knows anguish, anxiety, pain, happiness, positivity and joy, but it is also responsible for the thoughts that direct these emotions. This body is not always a reliable source of information for your emotional body, as the mind can play tricks on you and force you to believe things that may cause you unnecessary anguish. It may also give you false hope and lead you to believe in things that are not a reality, such as a love that is not returned to you by another or that people are persecuting you when they are not.

Follow these directions to let go of the trauma and emotions of the past:

* ❖ Look within yourself and talk to your body; ask it why it is in pain. It will always answer you, but you must be open to receiving the message.

* ❖ Locate the chakra, organ or part of the body where the emotion is held. See the colour and feel the emotion. Give yourself permission to release that which no longer serves you.

* ❖ Breathe in light as love and send it to the area. When you breathe out breathe out the pain, trauma or negative emotion.

* ❖ As you breathe out willingly release the pain and the trauma of the past to allow you to move freely into the future. Forgive those who have wronged you. If you find any of this to be difficult, ask Creator or your angel guides to help you in this request.

* ❖ Stay in the space and watch the colours change. Feel the emotion or trauma being released and give it up freely. Or, if you find this visualisation difficult, pass it to your angel guide as a ball of energy and watch them take it up to God's light.

* ❖ See it go from your aura, from you chakras and from your organs. See it go from the place in the body from which it stems, and send it with love on its way.

* ❖ When it is all gone, hold the intention of a healing. Breathe in the adamantine particles of creation with Creator's light and send it to the area that has had the release. See or feel it being healed and completely cleansed.

* ❖ Give thanks for the healing and zip up your aura. Ground your energy back into Mother Earth.

Of course, not all trauma and pain stems from a past life. What occurs in your current life at certain periods, whether it be in your childhood, adulthood, or old age, adds to your soul journey and to the emotions that are stored up in all of your four bodies. Follow the procedure I have described above and you will feel freer than you can ever remember.

Forgiveness is a gift that many who have suffered at the hands of others find difficult to bestow. This is because to forgive someone who has inflicted pain or sorrow seems, to the victim, to be allowing the perpetrator freedom from any responsibility of their actions. However, not to forgive is actually more harmful to you in the long term because the negative emotions attached to the memories remain harboured in your cells, organs, chakras and all four bodies, causing more emotional trauma which can then manifest as physical symptoms. To forgive all those who have transgressed upon you is to set yourself free from the memories that bind you to the past and that are preventing you from moving forward into the future. Forgiveness is your own redemption and salvation.

We must give thanks, however, for the lessons that we have learnt. Feeling emotions from joy to pain is an integral part of the human experience. When we have experienced loss, grief, hatred, and pain and, on the other side, joy, love, bliss, and happiness, our souls remember and use these lessons to evolve to higher realms of consciousness. We become able, as spiritual beings on the etheric plane, to empathise with our human counterparts which enables us to give assistance to them in a deeper and more meaningful way. Experience leads to understanding, and understanding leads to evolvement. Evolvement leads to enlightenment, and all paths lead to the light.

And so it is.

CHAPTER 12

Travellers

As spiritual beings we are all travellers in time and space. We travel between worlds and between dimensions. When we are in spirit our travelling knows no distance and no bounds — we think and we are there. We hold the intent and our energy is transported. We are not held back by fear or limitations. We hold the belief that we can create and therefore we do.

As human beings on Earth your spirit begins to forget what it has known in the spirit world, but your soul remembers. You feel held back by the distance between planets and between worlds and the size of the Universe holds you in complete awe. Yet, in your subconscious and in your dreams, your soul still travels. It meets with its masters and teachers on the Etheric planes to continue the lessons it began before birth into the human form.

The human form uses technology and skill to build vessels that will take it to explore outer space and beyond the solar system. Yet, in spirit, you have already mastered this exploration. If you could tap into the wisdom of your higher self, which is your subconscious guide, you would be shown the wondrous sights that, as a human, you can only ever hope to see, and of which only a select few will ever get to witness.

Think back to a time when you dreamt you were flying, or that you had left your body and were in a place away from your home. Believe this, it was not a dream but an actual occurrence! Your spirit left your body while you slept to continue its exploration on the Astral Plane. There are times in which you will be aware of these journeys and at other times you will not. Dreams are often adventures you have had when you were asleep. If you feel like you have been there, you probably have!

Astral travelling allows the spiritual body to explore and learn in ways that the physical body can never do. These lessons are important for your spiritual growth and are not to be feared. The sensation of leaving your body can indeed be disconcerting, but know that your spirit desires this freedom to soar into the realms because your physical body cannot. It is going home and meeting with its spiritual family, whether it be from a past life, another dimension or even another world.

It is also possible to travel to other times, dimensions and worlds in a meditative state and those who have been awakened do so for the benefit of themselves, others and the planet. The ability to see through the Third Eye is of great benefit in this endeavour along with the ability to trust in the messages one is receiving. To attempt to send your consciousness out into space and/or the unknown without at first connecting to a trusted source, such as the Creator, a master or an angel guide would be folly, however, for those who have not had the practise or the guidance to do so. Learning to meditate and direct your mind and intention with focus and clarity is a very good start to learning to traverse the universe or to time travel with accuracy and in safety. It is a big, wide spirit world out there, but the wonders of the universe, of the ethereal world and of your own Divine calling are at your fingertips when you are ready to explore them.

And so it is.

Chapter 13

Dreams

Your dreams are your subconscious mind's way of sifting through the debris of drama that occurs on the physical planes. Dreams are also the unconscious playground of your spirit as it journeys ever forth beyond the physical restrictions of your body. Dreams help you to work through the issues that are confronting your soul which need to be resolved and released to avoid causing undue emotional or physical stresses.

It is not always necessary for you to take your dreams literally, but there are those whose dreams are predictions of what is yet to come. Psychic predictions made in dreams are rare but do occur, and those who foresee the future in their dreams are gifted and should never take their gifts lightly.

Dreams are symbolic of thought and action. They may seem bizarre and surreal and many times they will be disjointed, but the messages, when interpreted correctly, can give much guidance to the dreamer. Your dreams are your contact with your Higher Self, which is your Christed-self and your connection to your Divine Blueprint. The messages are being told to you as they hold importance for you at the time. If you cannot resolve them they will continue to re-occur until you take heed. Recurring dreams must be taken seriously, as they hold the key to unlocking important information that will help you to improve situations in your waking hours. Behold the importance of your dreams, for many of them come from your soul.

If you cannot resolve the significance of symbols or events in your dreams, ask for guidance and help. You can ask the Creator or your guides to show you the way to receiving the answers you need in a more forthright manner. When you have asked for help you will receive it. You may suddenly just know the answer or another person will give you the message in a different way. Whichever way you receive it, your soul will know when it is resolved because your dreams will change.

Déjà vu is another manifest of the mind that is an attempt to remind the recipient that they are here both in the present and the past. The manipulation of time can happen because the universe does not operate on time at all, therefore it is possible to be living our past and future at the same time as our present. As confusing as this may seem, the phenomenon that is déjà vu is a sign that you are or have traversed time and that the events you are now witnessing are actually being re-lived. The reasons for this to occur may be two-fold: one is that you did not complete the lesson that was involved with this event in your life and you have come back to do so, or the second is that the significance of the place or event involved to you soul's purpose or learning is being revealed to you as a reminder and to realign all of your bodies with that reality.

Day-dreaming is another way that your Higher Self, your angel or spirit guides may contact you. You may suddenly see a vision or find yourself in a different reality. While these may or may not be grounded in truth, the messages that come from these manifestations are worth taking note of.

Dreams are important. Take notice of them, for they will help you to resolve the issues that are affecting you in this life, as well as giving you clues to issues that need resolving from lives you have previously lived.

And so it is.

CHAPTER 14

Training Your Mind to Follow Your Sacred Heart

Your mind is a great leader. It leads you to believe in mortality. It leads you to believe that science is the only explanation to the ways of the world and the structure of the universe. It speaks to you as common sense and reason and it gives you answers that may be found in books and which humans can comprehend in the physical realm.

Your mind houses your ego. It tries to tell you that materialism is important and that status promoting inequality is acceptable and justified. However, the ego serves the self. It ignores the fact that all souls are born equal in the eyes of God and it puts itself first. When you listen to your mind you are susceptible to the tricks that it plays on you. You will believe in the illusions of the material world and you will be caught up in the lies that have been spun by the great egos of the leaders of the world. In the state of the mind, the possibility that the opportunity to learn the lessons your soul has chosen to learn may be lost is great, because you have listened to the tricks of the mind and ignored the innermost knowing of your sacred heart.

Your sacred heart is your sacred space. It houses your soul and is your eternal connection to the *all*. When you sit within your sacred heart the influences of the mind are minimised and the true meaning of the situation at hand becomes apparent. In this sacred space your connection to Source is maximised, and the voice of God within will become crystal clear. The illusions of the physical world will be gone and the possibilities of the universe will be open to you. When you think from your Sacred Heart space you will have the best ability to remain in integrity, and any course of action you choose to make will be of the highest order. Follow these directions to think from your sacred heart-space:

❖ To find your sacred heart space, close your eyes and centre your thoughts on your breath.

❖ When you are feeling relaxed, bring your awareness to the space in your chest that is in front of your heart.

❖ Feel your energy building there, like a ball of beautiful white light, and, when you are ready, sit yourself in that light and breathe in the sacred light of God. For your light is God's light — there is no separation.

❖ Now, holding the intention of being in your sacred heart space, see a doorway open up before you. Enter this doorway and you will be in the innermost sanctum of your soul. It is the place where you can commune with the Creator and yourself in peace and tranquillity. The closeness you feel to Creator will feel sacred and will make you feel whole again. You will also just 'know' the answer to your problem without needing to think about it.

❖ Many people see colours, or one particular colour, when they are in their sacred heart-space; seeing a particular colour or pattern may enable to recognise when you are there. If you cannot 'see', you will feel the energy change around you, or you will feel a swelling of love in your heart-space that is overwhelmingly peaceful. This is your sacred space, your special place to be one with God, the universe and the *all*.

Your sacred heart is connected to your sacred mind and your sacred fire. This triad forms the basis of your Solar Power centre. As humans you may feel that esoteric and universal knowledge is beyond your reach, but when you activate your Solar Power centre you are reclaiming your Divine birthright and empowering yourself to acknowledge yourself as a co-creator in your own right.

Think with your heart, not your head. Begin to see yourself as a creator in charge and in control, not as a follower being controlled by a higher force. You are one with the Creator, the highest Source. You create your own reality with every thought and belief.

And so it is.

CHAPTER 15

The Higher Self

Your higher self is your etheric self — it holds the wisdom of your soul. It knows your soul journey and is your link to the etheric planes and universal knowledge. It is your sub-conscious mind in connection to and in harmony with your consciousness and your Christ-mind that knows more than you are aware of. If you have a psychic 'knowing', it comes from your Higher Self.

The wisdom of the higher mind is connected to Source. Its knowledge is that of the Creator of All-That-Is, as you are directly connected to Source and never separated. All you ever need to do is to connect to your Higher Self to know that you are at one with the Creator and the universe.

Your Higher Self is located above your crown. It resides there because it is of the etheric planes — it is in this world but not of it. It is your innermost thoughts and your innermost knowing. Your Higher Self is wise beyond your years and wise beyond this life.

Use your Higher Self's wisdom in times when an answer is beyond your realm of conscious knowing. You can tap into this wisdom by simply asking it. Ask your higher self to help you and to tell you the answer you seek in the following way:

❖ Close your eyes and connect with your Higher Self. See it as a beautiful ball of white light rotating slowly above your crown. If it is easier for you, invite your Higher Self to enter your conscious mind.

❖ Ask your question, clear your mind and wait for the answer to come. If there is no answer, perhaps you are not yet ready to know. Otherwise your mind may be cluttered and is blocking the answer; Clear it and try again. Be patient with yourself, for you have everything you need to know within your grasp and within your consciousness. All you need to do is to learn to access it.

❖ If it is still difficult, invite your Higher Self into your Sacred Heart space and feel, rather than know, the answer you seek.

❖ The answer may come as a thought, a feeling, a vision, a knowing… the more you are in touch with the way you receive psychic messages the easier it will be to interpret it.

Your Higher Self is possibly an aspect of one of your former lives, but this is not always the case. It may be a Master of the ages or it may be a newer soul-aspect. Wherever its origin, it is etheric in nature and your link to your own psychic gifts. Everyone who lives upon the Earth has the ability to be psychic; it is just a matter of awakening and tuning into the gifts that are rightly yours.

Do not be afraid to use etheric wisdom, for it is what you have come from and is your innermost knowing. Tap into your higher wisdom and discover your Super-Conscious mind that holds unspoken truths of the universe.

And so it is.

PART FOUR

THE ETHERIC REALMS

CHAPTER 16

The Planes of Existence

There are seven planes of existence in the universe. Humans exist in the Third Plane, but we use and work within all planes at the same time. Planes of existence are realms of consciousness that can be known or unknown. Whether man is consciously aware of his place amongst these planes or not, they exist and he is an existential part of them.*

Each plane of existence, apart from the Seventh Plane, abides by its own particular vows and commitments. Those who work or dwell within these planes will also be bound by them. Sometimes you will not notice any effects from being bound to a vow from a certain plane, but many of them can be extremely limiting or even dangerous to humans who dabble in things they consciously know not much about. The only way to be free from any vow or commitment from a particular plane is to work through the Creator of All-That-Is.

God is protection. His white light is truth and unconditional love. When you connect to God first and ask him your request for your highest and best, you will then be free to move amongst the planes and will not be bound by any of their particular laws. Those who practise religion connect with Creator when they pray. Those who practise Buddhism connect with the God in themselves, which is the same as connecting to the Creator. Those who practise no religion or who do not believe in God are in danger, however, of working in the energies of the lower planes and of being bound to the vows and commitments that are constituted within them.

The energy of each plane of existence is powerful and extremely healing. The beings that reside within some of the planes can be very helpful to the person requiring healing or assistance. These beings can provide opinions and advice and will always give assistance willingly and immediately. People working with angels or archangels, for instance, who reside in the Upper Fifth Plane, will feel very loved and, sometimes, instantly healed. Those working with Reiki or mystic healing, which is of the Fourth Plane, will find that they feel calm and renewed.

However, the lower planes of existence trade energies with the healer. There are conditions imposed upon the healer whereby a trade of energy or imposed restrictions on their healing powers will mean that they take on the energy of others. They may also be swayed by the opinions of beings who may not be working in the person's best interest. The forms of healing and assistance from these planes will be of a lower order and will therefore influence the energy that is exuded by the person using that plane for their purposes. They may become deluded by visions of power and begin to think that they are more powerful than others or, in contrast, they may feel that they cannot use the healing powers of their guides without needing to suffer or to go through immense hardship.

Be extremely wary of any healer who charges too much or who presents as the fount of all knowledge. If you feel uncomfortable with a person because they are judgemental, vindictive or egocentric, you may be sure that the plane of existence they are influenced by is not the Seventh Plane.

Always connect to the Creator of All-That-Is before embarking on any healing or energy work. Ask for assistance and healing for your or for others' highest and best. When you have connected with the Seventh Plane you will be free to work with the beings and elements of the lower planes without conditions.

What you believe you create — let no other being tell you that you are cursed or doomed, for this is only an attempt by them to assert power over you and to rob you of your own power. There is no judgement in the Seventh Plane, only love. When you work through the energy of the Creator you will be protected, and you will also be a protector.

And so it is.

---

* For more information on the planes of existence, see "Theta Healing, go up and work with God" (Stibal, 2011).

Chapter 17

Universal Laws and Knowledge

Universal knowledge is based on Spiritual Law. The Laws are written but they are also known. Even if this is the first time on Earth that you have heard about Spiritual Laws, your Higher Self knows of them and why they exist. The laws of the universe never change for they are living and breathing realms of consciousness that have their own vibrations, sounds, colours and thoughts. They are also written and bound in volumes that reside in the Akashic Records library on the Sixth Plane of Existence.

The laws abide by each other and they exist in unison. They are in each other and of each other. There are many laws that lie within other laws. They are complex and diverse, with many dimensions and layers to them. To understand the laws in all of their complexity is indeed a mammoth task and one that is not recommended, because their complexity causes them to be unfathomable to most.*

It is not the intention of this chapter to outline the laws or to explain them in any great detail. It is more useful for you to know that within each law there are by-laws and conditions that make each law unique to itself. The laws contain within them conditions for use that, if not abided by, will invoke other laws into action. Laws are not beliefs, for they reside in our consciousness as fact and are non-negotiable.

Laws control the elements and they control the revolving of the planets, moons and suns. They are the reason you stay grounded on the Earth and that you reincarnate again and again. They hold the soul accountable and they govern the agreements made between souls in the re-enactment of karma on the Earthly Planes. There is nothing that you do or know that is not governed by universal law. All beings, whether they are beings of light or human beings, are bound by spiritual law — not even the supreme source, Creator of All-That-Is, can transgress them. Laws are final and binding; all beings existing within the universe and on all planes of existence are bound by them.

When you go into the laws to ask for help you must be extremely careful of how you ask and what you ask for. The laws will always do your bidding, but they do not understand the minds of men and will take any command literally. They will not discern whether what you ask is for your highest and best unless you ask that it be so. As has been discussed, the best route to take when consulting the laws is through the Creator, for when you go to him first all consultation with the Sixth Plane will be through the Seventh and thus protected from any agreements which could compromise the quality of assistance given.*

Your soul and Higher Self knows the laws and how to abide by them. You will instinctively know if you have transgressed spiritual law because your soul will tell you — you will have a bad feeling, you may feel uncomfortable, or your beliefs may be challenged. Listen to your intuition when it comes to spiritual laws. If you are unsure of whether you are abiding by them or not, ask your higher self, pray to the Creator or meditate silently. It will be clear and you will know.

To abide by spiritual law is of the utmost importance, for transgression against any law will immediately invoke repercussions which will be swift and of more immense proportions than the original deed.

Universal knowledge is known by all souls living on Earth in different degrees, depending on the number of lives that have been lived and the quality of the lessons learned by each soul. All any person needs or wants to know about the universe is held as wisdom in their Higher Selves and can be accessed at any time. However, most humans lose touch with their Higher Selves and their link to other worlds and the ethereal kingdom soon after childhood.

There are different levels of human consciousness, all of them holding wisdom and knowledge. The human collective consciousness does hold knowledge but it is not reliable as it is tainted with human emotion and drama. The Christ Consciousness is the highest consciousness and is accessible to the person who has become spiritually aware though their Higher Self. In this consciousness the ego has become secondary to the need to serve and to achieve oneness with the Creator, the universe and the all.

Universal knowledge and wisdom is not just the knowledge of how the universe was created or why planets exist. It does encompass the laws as the laws explain and underpin everything there is to know about existence itself. There is much to be gained for the Earth when humans work through their Higher Self to apply etheric and universal wisdom, but those who are not in integrity can also use it to benefit themselves at the expense of the human race.

With the energies of Ascension becoming more intense and overwhelming for many, regaining the knowledge of how to step back into your Divine Blueprint and take back your power as Light Beings in a human body is highly recommended and will be hugely advantageous to each person who decides to do so. The positive ripple-effect out to society and Mother Earth cannot be overestimated. There are now many Lightworkers and Wayshowers ready to show the way, but meditation and raising your vibrations to become more tolerant of differences is the first step to connecting to the wisdom and knowledge that is available to you and part of your Divine birthright.

It is so.

---

* For more information on the Sixth Plane of Existence, see Stibal, V. (2011).

CHAPTER 18

The Universe

The universe is an unknown quantity to humans. It seems vast and never-ending, with too many elements left undiscovered. Beyond your solar system there are many other worlds and your scientists know of some of them. However, I am here to tell you that what you think of as aliens are actually related to you. In fact, many of you have lived lives on other planets in other solar systems!

As spiritual beings we can traverse the universe in an instant. There are no boundaries for a soul in its etheric state. Other worlds can be visited and incarnated upon, as Earth is not the only choice when it comes to reincarnation. Where a soul chooses to live is very much dependent on how evolved it is, the lessons it has yet to learn and where its soul family resides. A soul may choose to rest itself away from the density of the Earthly Plane for decades or even centuries and during this time it may go beyond the confines of this solar system to other worlds. These worlds could be where the soul originates from, or they could be places it has not been before. It matters not, as etheric souls are welcome in all corners of the universe, and the knowledge they gain is invaluable for helping others upon their path.

Earth is not the only planet that contains life in the universe, but it is the only planet where its intelligent forms, human beings, have learned to hate. There are no other planets in the universe where the life forms treat each other with such disrespect and disregard. This is the biggest lesson for the human race at this time: to learn to live in harmony, love and peace, with total acceptance of each other and of your differences.

The universe revolves around love. God, the Creator of All-That-Is, loves all who live on Earth unconditionally. In your etheric state you are beings of love. You treat each other with accord, respect and reverence and you accept all, judging nothing. You are peaceful and you radiate light and love. There is no other recognisable state of *being* in the universe. Hatred and war are not ways of being — they are states of *doing* and disequilibrium which can bring nothing but unhappiness and karma.

The Earth has ascended to return humans to their etheric state of *being*, that is, one of peace, love and total harmony. Mother Earth has shaken off her coat of woe and has risen above the Third Dimension. She now sits in her higher state. Those of you who choose to join her will soon know what it is to live as beings in other worlds do: in peace, harmony, and a state that radiates light and love out to the world and beyond. We in the etheric realms, who are watching this change, are overwhelmed with joy and love for you as you embrace this new journey with Mother Earth.

Embrace the changes before you as you live upon Mother Earth in this time of transition. Feel the energies shifting from ones of negativity, control and fear to that of tolerance, peace, love and oneness. Reject the past teachings of doctrine that you are separate from each other and from the Creator, and embrace the unity of oneness in total love-energy. Join with us in the etheric realms as we bring the Earth into alignment with the rest of the universe. The ways of the universe are now more open to you than ever before. Recognise your spiritual self and rejoice in the harmonies as all planes of existence merge together to bring oneness and peace to your souls. Then you will live life on Earth as was always intended and as in all other worlds — in total harmony, unity and unconditional love-energy.

We are all one with God and with each other.

It is so.

CHAPTER 19

Knowing and Living the Truth

You know everything you need to know about the universe and how it works. You know every spiritual law and you know how the world was created. You know God's eternal love and, when you were born, you shone his light like a beacon. That light burns in each and every one of you in your sacred heart, but some of you have lost touch with your higher selves and thus have forgotten what you already know.

Many of you on Earth are now being awakened to the higher truth of your existence. You are beginning to see things as they really are and, as the density of the Third Dimension falls away, you see things from a higher perspective. You also start to remember who you are in spirit and why you came to Earth in the first place. The fallacies that society has indoctrinated in you will be difficult to shift but, over time, the higher truths of the universe will always prevail in your consciousness.

Fear not the truth and embrace the challenges that come with facing facts that were previously not held in your belief systems. No journey is complete without learning and learning only comes when mistakes have been made and belief systems shaken. There is no shame in realizing that what you once held up as truth is actually a fallacy. It is all part of the experience of being human. Pride is but the ego which wishes to rule when, in fact, the results of upholding one's pride can only be a missed opportunity to know one's truth, and for others to know the true you.

The truth will always come to light no matter how long it has been hidden. It is better to fear the lies, for they can only bring about darkness and disrepute. Integrity comes with upholding the truth in the face of adversity, whereas shying away from truth is a sure way to bring oneself into karma and disarray.

There have been many mistruths told upon your Earth and man has come to believe and live them as gospel. God has been aligned with religion and upheld as judge and jury, when neither is the case. God the Creator is the essence of unconditional love and he has no affiliation with any religion that has ever been created upon the Earth. Religion is nothing but the creation of man, designed to allow him to justify and explain a phenomenon he does not understand. What is there to understand about love? Why does it need to be so hard when loving yourself and your fellow man as one with the Creator is all that has ever been required of you?

Living in a state of love is living in the light. When you see all in this context the rest will fall away as trivial and irrelevant. When you live in God's light you are living in your own light. When you love yourself you love God — you become one with Him, with Mother Earth and the all. In this state, which is that of the Fifth Dimension, you will know what it is to love and to just be. In this state you will be aligned with the truth of the universe, and the drama and illusion of the Earthly Plane will lose its validity. In this state of ascension the human form will return to its ethereal state, and the Earth will begin to know harmony and peace as it has never known before. It can be done.

Know the truth, live it, and it will occur.

You are loved, you *are* love and we are one.

It is so. So be it.

I AM Master Saint Aloysius.

Blessings, love and light to you.

BIBLIOGRAPHY

Cochrane, V. (2013). *Raising the energies of mother earth towards and after ascension 2012: The highest truth.* Second Edition, Australia, Victoria Cochrane Publications.

Hay, L. (2004). *You can heal your life.* NY, USA: Hay House, Inc.

Stibal, V. (2011). *Theta Healing: Introducing an amazing healing modality.*

Ammon, Idaho: Rolling Thunder Publishing.

Powell, D.; Powell, Y. (2011). *Jesus and Mary Magdalene: The Eternal Heart of Love: Volume 1.* Available as an e-book or to purchase from www.circleoflight.net

Kribbe. P. (2013). *Auriela: The Jeshua Channelings.* www.jeshua.net Retrieved May 14, 2012.

ABOUT THE AUTHOR

Victoria Cochrane is a psychic channel, medium and spiritual healer who lives on the North West coast of Tasmania with her husband, Richy. She is also a literacy specialist and classroom teacher. Victoria began this spiritual journey in 2008 when she did a beginner's spiritual development course. She has since become a Reiki Master and an Advanced Theta® Healer, and is a teacher in her own right, running her own spiritual development courses to help people to follow their own spiritual path. Her psychic gifts include channelling, past life healings and mediumship, specializing in helping people to release past trauma in order to step into their own gifts. This is her second book, which is a sequel to her first book, Raising the Energies of Mother Earth Towards and After Ascension 2012: The Highest Truth (Balboa Press, 2013) which was released in February 2013 and reprinted in 2016. Her third book, The Alignment of the Universe: Messages from Other Worlds was first published in 2015 and was reprinted in 2016.

www.victoriacochrane.com

Lightning Source UK Ltd.
Milton Keynes UK
UKHW041428310722
406630UK00001B/9